Take a Hike, Snoopy!

LITTLE SIMON
An imprint of Simon & Schuster Children's Publishing Division
1230 Avenue of the Americas
New York, New York 10020

Manufactured in the United States of America
First Edition
2   4   6   8   10   9   7   5   3   1

The Library of Congress has cataloged the paperback edition as follows:

Katschke, Judy.
Take a hike, Snoopy! / adapted by Judy Katschke.
p. cm. — (Ready-to-read)
"Peanuts."
"Based on the comic strips by Charles M. Schulz."
Summary: The world famous Beagle Scout takes his eager bird troops on a camping
and hiking trip that turns out to be very different from what Snoopy planned.
ISBN 0-689-84938-9 (alk. paper)(pbk.)
ISBN 0-689-85262-2 (lib ed)
[Hiking—Fiction. 2. Camping—Fiction. 3. Scouts and scouting—Fiction.
4. Beagle (Dog breed)—Fiction. 5. Dogs—Fiction. 6. Birds—Fiction.] I. Title. II. Series.

PZ7.K15665 Tak 2002

[E]—dc21   2001038491

Take a Hike, Snoopy!

Based on the comic strips
by Charles M. Schulz
Adapted by Judy Katschke
Art adapted by Nick and Peter LoBianco

Ready-to-Read

Little Simon
New York London Toronto Sydney Singapore

The world-famous Beagle Scout leader was taking his troop on a nature hike and had plans for an overnight camp-out.

"We will separate and meet back here in forty-five minutes," Snoopy said to his scouts.

"This will teach and promote self-reliance," Snoopy continued. But the birds came rushing back and gathered around Snoopy's feet—in less than five minutes!

"That was a short forty-five minutes," Snoopy said.

"Just for that," Snoopy said, "we'll try it again."

"And I don't want to see anyone hanging around my feet!" he ordered.

Snoopy sighed as the birds crowded onto his Beagle Scout hat. At least they listened to *some* of what he said!

Finally the campers were ready to roll.

"We start our hike in exactly one hour," Snoopy told his troop. "I suggest you get your gear together right now!"

The scouts ran off to get ready for their overnight camp-out.

Snoopy thought the birds would pack food, tents, and compasses. He rolled his eyes when he saw Woodstock return with golf clubs, and Harriet carefully holding her angel-food cake with seven-minute frosting. Snoopy wondered if the birds understood camping in the wilderness!

But Snoopy knew the drill. He knew
what gear to pack for a long hike.

"Does everyone have a full canteen?"
Snoopy asked. Woodstock, Harriet, Conrad,
and Bill checked their backpacks.

"You can't go on a long hike without
water!" Snoopy reminded them. "Always
remember that water is our friend!"

Unless it pours on your camping trip.
"Thanks, friend!" Snoopy gurgled.
They should have packed umbrellas!

When the rain stopped, the Beagle Scouts marched on.

"All right, troops," Snoopy said. "We're entering tall grass country!" The scouts gulped when they saw the grass. It was taller than they were.

"This could mean queen snakes!"
warned Snoopy.

"I suggest that we walk in single
file," he told the troop.

The scouts hopped to it . . .

. . . right on top of Snoopy's hat!
  "Okay," Snoopy sighed. "We'll
walk vertical file."

Meanwhile, Charlie Brown was worried about his dog.

"Snoopy went on a camping trip," he told Lucy. "And he never came back. I wonder if he's lost."

"Of *course* he's lost!" Lucy said. "That stupid beagle couldn't find his nose on his face! He couldn't find his hands in his mittens! He couldn't find the ears on his head!"

"I don't think he's *that* helpless," Charlie Brown said. "After all, he is a Beagle Scout, you know."

Lucy gave it a thought. Then she heaved a big sigh. Maybe Charlie Brown was right. Maybe Snoopy wasn't lost after all.

But back in the wilderness, Snoopy *was* feeling a little lost. As he led his troop over a bridge, he gulped. "This bridge must be a thousand feet high!"

The scouts had to see for themselves.
They leaned over the side.

"Be careful!" Snoopy warned Woodstock.
"What would happen if you fell?"

"Nothing," Woodstock said. "We can fly!"

So birds can fly.

"Big deal," Snoopy muttered as they crossed the bridge. *He* was a World War I Flying Ace!

And he was still the leader—doggone it!

When it came time to build camp,
Snoopy gave the orders.

"Okay, troops," he said. "Here's
where we'll spend the night."

"We'll be here for a couple of days,"
Snoopy added, "so make it a happy place."
Snoopy left to fetch some firewood. But
when he came back, he was in for a surprise!

Camp was not exactly
what he had expected!

The scouts had set up a Ferris wheel and a merry-go-round!

The next day Snoopy was leading his troop through the woods when he heard the sweetest sound.

He had to go home! They packed up and hurried to Charlie Brown's house.

Charlie Brown was glad to see Snoopy, but he was also surprised.

"You were out far beyond all civilization," Charlie Brown said, "and suddenly you heard five chocolate-chip cookies calling you?"

Snoopy and his scouts grinned.

After everyone had enjoyed the
cookies, Charlie Brown had another
treat for Snoopy.

"Guess what, Snoopy?" he asked.

Snoopy looked at the round-headed
kid. Charlie Brown was holding a tent
and pegs!

"Mom said I could pitch a tent and sleep outside tonight!" Charlie Brown said excitedly. He started setting up his tent.

That's great! Snoopy thought.
He charged into the house—straight
to Charlie Brown's room!

Snoopy snuggled under the covers.
"I'm glad he's happy!" Snoopy sighed.

Camping is cool.
And so is being a Beagle Scout.
But *real* happiness is a nice, warm bed!